Mike McGurk is British born and bred but has lived most of his adult life in Norway. His present home is in a small village on an island off the west coast of Norway. He is married to the Norwegian author, Solfrid Sivertsen, and has two children and two grandchildren. Mike has made a living as a painter and song lyricist whilst doing a bit of teaching in between times in order to make ends meet. This collection of poems marks his return to where it all started…a return to poetry.

To Colin Baxter, kindred spirit and 'partner in crime' ever since our paths first crossed in Weston-Super-Mare back in the early sixties.

Michael Deegan McGurk

MEANWHILE BACK AT THE NEST

AUSTIN MACAULEY PUBLISHERS™
LONDON • CAMBRIDGE • NEW YORK • SHARJAH

Copyright © Michael Deegan McGurk 2023

The right of Michael Deegan McGurk to be identified as author of this work has been asserted by the author in accordance with sections 77 and 78 of the Copyright, Designs and Patents Act 1988.

All rights reserved. No part of this publication may be reproduced, stored in a retrieval system, or transmitted in any form or by any means, electronic, mechanical, photocopying, recording, or otherwise, without the prior permission of the publishers.

Any person who commits any unauthorised act in relation to this publication may be liable to criminal prosecution and civil claims for damages.

A CIP catalogue record for this title is available from the British Library.

ISBN 9781398481589 (Paperback)
ISBN 9781398481596 (ePub e-book)

www.austinmacauley.com

First Published 2023
Austin Macauley Publishers Ltd®
1 Canada Square
Canary Wharf
London
E14 5AA

Tables for Two

in a quayside coffee shop
she flounders
barbed hook
torturing her mouth
into witless sound

at tables for two
or more
the black-backed gulls
are perched
shoving sandwiches aside
shrieking for guts

she ties a scarf
over heaving gills
frantic
piscine eyes
search the flock
for one
to carry her
flapping to the water's edge

to throw her in
to sink
to swim
to oblivion

Swinging Doors

endless beer
and anecdotes
in and out
of countless throats
waiters
trapped in timeless days
of swinging doors
and balanced trays

no sign
of what was done
or said
of glasses raised
to wet the heads
of those
now grown and sitting here
desperate
to drown *their* fears
in
endless beer
and anecdotes
in and out

of countless throats
and waiters
trapped in timeless days
of swinging doors
and balanced trays

Suppose

suppose some boy
should find the dike
had sprung a leak
but so unlike
the fairy tale
he could not brave
the pain and cold
or stop the wave
nor from his place outside the fold
see anyone to save

and what if he
should share the fact
with men of cloth
who dared not act
but washing hands
in Pilate style
just answered him with pious smile
salvation's there for everyone
but God has left the building son

fingers weaken
hearts can burst
and bid the ocean do its worst
just let the waters enter in
to wash away all sense of sin

say such a boy
should lose his hold
would his story still be told?

The Song of the Whale

derelicts
don't drown in sorrow
like stranded whales
they flounder
close to shore
pressing
brainless heads
against tomorrow
and doors
that will not open anymore

deep
in bloated darkness
swings the eye
once salved by ocean swell
now tinder dry
observing
fellow mammals
all day long
spouting
high-pitched sound
some call it song

Worlds Away

worlds away
too far for feet
too bright for day
too dark for sleep
the wingless fall

guided by a neon light
rejecting wings
and mocking flight
they crawl

near at hand
too short for years
a sense of loss
too deep for tears
and
mouthing sounds
too close for ears
they call

With Wire Brush

some busy
boiler-suited arm
has placed
two concrete pipes
on end
to curb the flow
of dry-stone wall
and punctuate
a wood

with wire brush
and iron will
the keeper of the gate
defends
his pocket Parthenon
dictates
to moss and alga
where to grow

but when the back
is turned
to clay

and working hand
to idle bone
a lichen robe
of green and grey
exalts the concrete pipe
to stone

To the Quick

young fingers should not
lend their limber days
to fondling
harmless stones
but blindly probe
and scathe their tips
down to the quick
on flint and granite braille
and fumbling
lose their way
inside volcanic rock
discarding…and rediscovering
forever splitting stone
in vicious search
of fossil truth

smooth stones
should rest
high up on pensive beaches
unashamed
in patient mountain streams
or in the sagging pockets of old men

who
dreaming now
of cliff-face climbs
and fiery lava flow
may lock their grip
on gathered pebbles
so they
though ominous
as petrified full stops
can
with their smoothness
reassure
loosen
the stiffening hand…steady the loosening grip

The Guardian

I'm the guardian of wisdom
my mind is at ease
though the doors are so many and small
I lock and unlock them with my set of keys
to enter it's me you must call
I carry them with me
and fight for the right
to hold forth about nothing at all

Tiger, Tiger...

tiger, tiger burning none too bright
with broken claw and silent roar
unfit to roam the jungle of the night
but give him love and he is yours

tiger, tiger prowling in a cage
with heavy heart and weary paw
his only crime he dares not act his age
forgive him this and he is yours

tries to be wild
tries to be tame
tries to live down and up to his name
he is no fool
he is not wise
but he sees the fear in your eyes

"Wild"...panics like the desperate child who cannot find its mother
"Tame"...keeps whispering any name whilst longing for another

tiger, tiger lying at your feet
with injured pride and battle sores
just be his shelter from the jungle heat
soothe his pain and he is yours

Three Sketches from Oslo

Looking back
so many naked canvases
were stretched to sheep-bell sounds
so many fumbled promises
were painted out of bounds
and so many bits of best-work-yet…
were just stabbings in the dark
triggered by his desperate need
to leave some kind of mark

Listening now
they're trying to tell me something
it's out there loud and clear
between the mouth that's moving
and this deafened ear

Getting it right
I'll weigh every word when I see them
not shoot from the hip when I don't
I'll run with the hounds…try to be them
but hunt with the hunter I won't

The Glacier

up here
all is steered
by the whispering
of ice
in motion on
this ancient floor

but with a moan
liquefied stone
breaks free
and seeks a way home
longing for some
distant shore

take me along
teach me the song
that kindles and drives
the drift of our lives
help me to flow
with the melting of snow
down to the sea

this done
I would run
with rivers
and be fearless
though I was heading for
the desperate leap
and the roar of the falls
would hush timid calls
to sleep

take me along
teach me the song
that kindles and drives
the drift of our lives
help me to flow
with the melting of snow
down to the sea

The Forester

only this
and nothing more
a past at rest
a void before

an idle axe
a pile of logs
his thoughts out bounding
with the dogs
balanced on their weaving backs
scenting out the hidden tracks

through the thicket
past the pine
deaf to dogma
blind to sign
ploughing purple as they go
circling in the fjord below
there to soothe the throbbing paw
close to drowning
close to shore

senses homed on fish that leap
pierce the quiet
find the deep
rings betraying what has been
man and dog
a single scene

the fading ring
the echoed bark
deliberately
he makes no mark

The Fisherman

he wished
he could fish
in the lake
but be sure
that the wishing
the fishing
were the same
simple
pure

and when the desire
to be somewhere higher
came over him
could
unwish the wish
uncatch the fish
and just climb
to a place
where last year he'd planted
and uproot…yet save
his trees of discontent

and plant them again
and again
for the gutted fish
grilled on glowing coals
harbouring a secret wish
to smell like teeming shoals
trapped
in a blazing forest

The Crush

her presence
steers
the rise and fall
of glass to lips
disturbs
a central-heated fly

hair is flicked
away from eyes
that long
to look
into hers

coyness
drums the tabletop
candles studied
moved replaced
but she's away
flirting
with the fly

confused
he flicks his hair again
curses flight
turns to wax
and
hangs his despairing chorus
on the bones
of her laughter

Take Up the Slack

what are they for
the parrot-fashion names we treasure
what have they done
to deserve so much more
don't ask us when
or why we thought it wise to measure
all that drifted to our door

our
eyes spying
tongues tying
knots and covering tracks
playing tricks we never learned
lives touching
minds clutching
at straws that are breaking the backs
of those teachers' ticks we never earned
take up the slack
keep up the act

why do we play
our game of mending-the-unbroken

the big giveaway
is when pieces are found
where do we pay
for speaking the unspoken
what do we say
out of sight and sound

our
eyes spying
tongues tying
knots and covering tracks
playing tricks we never learned
lives touching
minds clutching
at straws that are breaking the backs
of those teachers' ticks we never earned
take up the slack
keep up the act

Sunlit

the day outside
and all the days before
shone through the window
at her back
crowned her hair
but hid her face
manhandled her
through time and space
the woman and the child
were one
and I sat stunned
and out of reach
and wished the hurt
she now relived…undone
I held my breath
to match her grief
and sat there
wishing I could calm the child
and say
come here
I'll take the hurt away

Standing-Room Only

odourless cobbled street
with your picture-book houses
cling to your mountain
one of seven
Bergen's pride

may your cable car
on its climb
through evergreens
become
a double-decker
with standing-room only
and may the rising sap
of spruce and pine
forget its mission
unfurling leaves
of oak and elm

let me see
a square box
of red brick
with turquoise doors

and useless loft
in a sea-side town

let me be a boy again
in a cockney arcade
feeling for a while
a fistful of cold
old pence
waiting to be fed
into fateful one-armed slots

Somewhere

somewhere
between
the push-chair father's
foolish gaze
of swollen pride
and
the naked sweep
of a mother's eye
from her own
to another's offspring
lies a code

somewhere
wrapped
in awful
back-to-back silence
served up
as after-dark punishment
lodged between
logistics
and enlightenment
lies a code .... I long to crack

Perfection

perfection
picks
the cleanest of all holes
guided
by its power to disown
inflicting shafts of light
on cowering souls
it revels
in the sight
of naked bone

no chance to
reinforce
the fragile skin
or lower eyes
to signal the retreat
no point in
waging battle from within

the cut is clean
the exit wound
so neat

Painting Classes

fifth floor
going down
Senor Ibanez
and four old ladies
in a lift
descending from the Andes
from the council-coloured classroom
leaving on each floor
canvas offerings
here…a deer grazing in greyish green
there…impossible logs lying
houses barns tilting
flying
away from sheep
scratched into the granite beyond

down
down to the street
to meet an indifferent Nordic sun
as lukewarm as his "same-time-next-week"
for the Inca in him knows

that the final eclipse
has already begun

Onto the Razor Rocks

a summer evening
left ajar
to let
the scented breeze
of wheatfields
brush his cheek
and fill the sail
of yachting fathers
at the bar
not obliged by blood
but buying rounds

urging him
to forfeit
shoreline safety
for a stake
in auburn
horseback daughters
bathed in lattice light
making
breaking promises
of love

a summer evening
open wide
the horseless girls
with flaxen hair
and lodestar eyes
steer boyish fathers
safe at sea
onto the razor rocks
in silver bays

trying to equate
the scenes
he feeds them
one by one
into the eye
hoping optic nerve…and brain
will do the rest

Now and Then

now and then
behind the rows
of pearly teeth
and trendy clothes
and in between the customers
in mirror-tiles
the spotlights pierce the shadows
and she sees

now and then
she senses that she's being watched
through steel-rimmed glass
and weighed
and being found too light
by those
who think like crows in flight

now and then
while gaolers rest
flocked in sleep
in cuckoos' nests

(dreaming of her painted claws)
she stretches out her gaudy wings.......and soars

No Common Dream

with table knife and fumbling craft
I carved my frog a driftwood raft
for every flash of blade in hand
some portion of his life I planned

we stood a while just him and me
before I sent him off to sea
away from stagnant pond and noise
of factories and jam-jar boys

the world his oyster to explore
both for himself and me ashore
I think he waved as if to say
he never would forget this day

we had our moment on the beach
but life had lessons still to teach
me on the sorrows and the joys
we heap on those we make our toys

my good intentions led to hell
for by and by on a sea of shell
I found the raft washed out of reach
of ocean swell and seagull screech

nearby my frog lay stretched and dry
with crucifixion in his eye

there is for all our schemes and ploys
no common dream for frogs and boys
and with him died a precious part
that is still missed by adult heart

Millimetre-Moves

grasping gods and galaxies
with such apparent ease
we make our millimetre-moves
and dare to hope we'll please

Meanwhile Back at the Nest

fledgling
full of worm and word
force-fed
to the brink
of woven straw and clay
anticipates
with feeble heart
and wing
the plunge

redundant
insect-hunters
fill the void
with instruments
to catch
the cosmic whisper
trust
that space and silence
mute the sound
of feathered bone
and beak
to ground

Just Another Jogger

just another jogger
fashion-wrapped
pounding tarmac
running on the spot
at traffic lights
counting steps and heartbeats
until…she snaps…
stops
and then…
strolls off in protest
shedding selfies
as she goes
whilst we……
in nearby coffee shops
pass the time
with anti-stress
colouring books
to the flow
of cafe latte
and feel no need to flinch
or be alarmed
but choose to brand

what we have seen
as her gift
to mindfulness

It Swoops Unseen

beyond observer's books
and climbing boys
there nests a bird
that only takes
to wing
to prey
on feeble-minded men
designed for toil
and useful days
but who stand too long
and gaze

gathering sunlight at its tail
it swoops unseen and strikes
with song caresses
ear and mind
while talons grip
the heart
and choke all talk
this bird
part nightingale
part hawk

I'd Be Content

if by chance or sleight of hand
my role in the eternal plan
were that of cat and not of man
I'd lie just where you're lying now
praising life with my meows

I'd be content to spend my days
curled up before the fire's blaze
moving only when the chill
of winter left the window sill

I'd slink about selecting laps
demanding food but scorning scraps
and throttle starlings in mid-song
unvexed by thoughts of right or wrong

but what if man decided that
I was a one-too-many cat
and the hand that stroked my back
should point the gun or tie the sack

I'd rather own the desperate paw
clawing at life's closing door
and take my last look at the sky
rather this than meet the eye
of a waiting child and falsely say
that their dearest friend had run away

I Know...

I know
that wiser men have been
that many will be born
I know
that countless bulls will charge
while others hold the horns

I know
that costumes others shape
will line up to be worn
and stage-blood find its way to smear
my crown of plastic thorns

I know
my fear of emptiness
and all that it might spawn
makes me fill my heart so full
there's no place left to mourn

I know
you know
that all I know

about this life I love
is all of this…but even though…
is none of the above

House-Building with a View

egged on
by south westerly winds
four slender elms
cross swords
between me
on site and the silver bay

blades slash
my sense of purpose
sways with the trees
but
in the heat of the duel
a cormorant cries
from a black pine-clad isle
beyond all this

and
for a moment
the sea-bird's call
and my half-built wall
both make some sort of sense

Guard Duty

I'll grant you
that I'd had a few
but toed the line
uninfluenced
between the sleeping children's beds

sobered by the late-night news
I stood a while
to guard their sleep
to stroke their hair
an extra time

and then
refolding them
to the foetal lie
I drew a leaden quilt
about their world

Epitaph

unable to attend
the polo-necked vicar
sends an email
on the properties of dust
to the graveside
in the name
of the father
the mourners ask
hardware
software is thy sting
and press delete

Depth of Field

there are those who claim
that the camera's aim
is to rob us of our soul
by stealing light
from us our might
gets sucked into a hole

and then shrunk in size
the spirit dies
a slow and awful death
starved of air it
withers there
until its final breath

but I think you'll find
that the simple minds
who think this is the case
are the none-too-bright and
unenlightened
members of our race

please don't quote
those lines I wrote
I'll try to walk the walk
adjust the lens
and make amends
for loose and foolish talk

it's so dark and cold
with just me to hold
where others ought to be
to awake and find
that my walls are lined
with no one else but me

must live for a while
with no selfie-smile
on a stick to help me show
what I'm about
behind the pout
where others must not go
and just eat the meals
my smartphone steals
from underneath my nose
and breathe the air
before I "share"
with you and faceless Joe´s

I hereby claim
that the smartphone's aim
is to rob us of our soul
by stealing light

from us our might
gets sucked into a hole
and shrunk in size
the spirit dies a slow and awful death
starved of air
it withers there
and draws its final breath

PS

After having completed this poem I came across a declaration, made by a prominent member of the Roman Catholic Church, stating the following:

And I quote:

"There are now more souls trapped within the confines of smartphone and digital camera memory cards than the Church has placed in Limbo, Purgatory, Heaven and Hell combined in the entire course of its existence!"

Caravan

heart cocooned in luscious leaves
of liquid green
and eyes still clutching
at the fading light
of desert stars once seen
he lashes blocks of salt
upon his back
and spreading toes
he treads the molten land
is swallowed by the shimmering air
becomes the sand

Bernadette

time heals
they'd said
but in a drawer
he'd signed
and sealed in grief
a tiny pair of shoes
he found
cut short the cure
released
an old woman
who lived in
one two come buckle my
hail Mary quite contrary
mother of a god
who has so many children
that he cannot move
in more mysterious ways
or
comfort fathers
who
left without nursery rhyme
or reason

choke on coined phrase
and are defeated by
a pair of shoes

At Some Dim Point

what became
of hands
that stroked
the baby's head
and
to cries of don't let go
steadied the tilt
of a two-wheeled world
or kept
the panic-stricken chin
above the waves

hers
found new things to hold
to tend to
and to stroke

his
at some dim point
let go
since no one
had said not to

he
let hands drop
to impotence
stirring only
on and off
to search
for ice-cream pennies
or
to wave

Word Came

and word went round that it was time
for us to walk erect
in order to be worthy of
the gift of intellect

with a minimum of insight
but prouder by the day
we now make sense or nonsense
of all that we survey

in hoisting up the spine and brain
some part was sold or lost
our eulogies are all in vain
we can but count the cost

I see my dogs and know they bear
a sorrow shrunk in size
to fit the range of timid heart
the scope of human eyes

and at their passing…unashamed
with stupid head-to-head
remembering how we roamed untamed
I'll howl what can't be said

Afraid of Knives, Are We?

he could have cut
the navel cord
himself
retied it when he felt
his life blood
being sapped

afraid of knives
the suckling took the strain
learned to live
with elastic

postnatal checks
reveal the cord end
firmly tied
to a swing door
marked maternity
and
a mother who
has left
no forwarding address

51, St Agnes

I am taking my leave of a childhood
while I choke on a piece of a dream
though I try to find cheer in an echo
my laughter returns as a scream

I must say my goodbyes to a building
must leave every room as it stands
closing each door like a surgeon
while a life slips away from my hands

under the weight of a sorrow
I stoop and I drop to one knee
then lifting my scalpel I carve out
a name in the hope it is me

A Mother's Eyes

that look
unfamiliar but hers
one frozen moment
camera caught
non maternal
defiantly innocent
open wide to the elements
long before us

her eyes
seeking out unimagined days
sweeping over countless
unwritten pages
still young enough to believe
that looking and seeing
were the same
the eyes of a child
peering out from behind
Greta Garbo-Like sockets
thrilled by the sight
of an untouched future

no footprints to follow
long before us

our mummy-to-be
hanging on her Allan's arm
invincible
in love
sill free
to survey vast landscapes
still believing
that the world was her oyster
and that life
would follow
one step behind
long before us

but living blended
light and dark
to confuse her days
leaving her no space
to breathe
too much too little
meted out
to trick the eye
to curb its sweep
make landscapes
treacherous to tread
but still she saw
trusted in the inner eye
and by its light
she made her moves

and kept us safe
when last we looked into her eyes
we saw that she was full of days
that Life had lit
and doused
so many times
that she now longed
for lids to close
(too soon for us)
couldn't wait to link her arm in his… in their's… and say I came

now we see
she must be more
than a mother missed by children
grieving their own brand of loss
that we let her
again become
young Lizzie
in or out of the frame
for only then can we mourn her
all the rest is just us

Bitter Taste

a slice of life a piece of cake
pick and choose and fill your plate
or eat the crumbs that others make
this is what we're told
grin and bear the bitter taste
join the queue the table's laid
fill your plate no time to waste
falter and you're sold

you are special you are blessed
bite off more than you can chew
disregard the other guests
this feast is set for you
just take the silver platter
and help yourself to all you need
no one minds or matters
or ever calls it greed

Days Run into One

as white as black in dead of night
as forceful as a feather's flight
though we try with all our might
as cool as lava when it moves
as free as needles in their grooves
we don't question what it proves

as hard as snowflakes in the sun
we melt and when we start to run
have to say what's done is done
as empty as a crowded room
we fill ourselves from crib to tomb
address the envelope to whom it may concern

as black as innocence we try
as light as lead to pass them by
the gifts intended for our eye
as warm as ice as soft as nails
gentle breezes howl like gales
and rip apart our flimsy sails

as blind as sight as false as real
as loud as silence we can feel
is ours to borrow not to steal
balanced on the edge of knives
as short as time as long as lives
we try to work with what arrives
survive

Greyhounds

blind to the foolish schemes of men
to the sterling load they bear
the canine bankers flee the trap
when baited by the hare

of all mankind's four-footed friends
none strains the friendship more
nor in pursuit of favour wends
home on a crueller paw

no word or sign is used to urge
the lung to fill the heart to beat
unleashed they balance on the verge
of triumph and defeat

I long to know the stainless force
that sears into a creature's frame
and makes it that it can divorce
the stakes yet run the same

Hardware

hardware
software
everywhere
who cares
mother dares
father tries
time flies
fast forward

best-dressed
paying guest
feel blessed
sell dear
buy cheap
fast lane
cancel sleep
let acid reign
numb pain
how could you

stroke me
curse me
choke me
nurse me
love or abhor me
just don't ignore me
let us meet
and find our feet
or failing this
press delete

Me Myself...

I don't give a monkey's
for winos and junkies
take the whole lot
and just dump 'em at sea
bus and cab drivers
a whole bunch of skivers
who work up a sweat
just by stirring their tea
nurses and teachers
are second rate creatures
their constant complaining
a strain on the nerves
fashion designers
and out-of-work miners
along with male dancers
a right bunch of pervs
and talking of shirkers
take bosses... and workers
and vicars and surgeons
and the money they earn
whether lefties or righties
they're so high and mighty

I've forgotten far more
than they'll ever learn
oysters and lobsters
Italian mobsters
and Mother Theresa
it's all foreign crap
and jocks with their sporrans
although they're not foreign
along with the paddies
are all on the tap…

but that's enough about me…tell me about yourself!

Moving North

it used to be
that desert days
with Dali shadows
would sweat things
to a head

but moving north
the days were
chipping ice from Norwegian slipways
attempting to release
the impatient galleon
that stood on crutches
embarrassed as red lead
and dreaming of the sun

laughing men built fires 'round the keel
and lifting ear flaps in salute
wrote messages on the hull.

when at last
the ship slid sighing
to the sea

we watched degraded icebergs
follow
without question
their master
to warmer days
and whispered promises
of nonexistence

Note from Home

so sorry
mummy
daddy
sir
miss
wife's gone
taken children
I promise
to try harder
tomorrow
yours sincerely
a clever (could-do-better)
boy

Stocktaking

as supervisors took stock
of a day's cornered crumbs
and money
leather pouched
was stashed away
I saw him
small and wire-rimmed
clutching at his change
fade through glass sliding doors
into the duffle-coated night

The Path

no more sorrow
shall be left unspoken
all the while hearts and minds
lie about me broken

no more closed eyes
must stop me seeing
and no sign shall point the way
when I'm set on fleeing

let me linger here
with all that I have found
and let my voice be more
than never-ending streams of sound

no more shall pictures dim and die
before they've reached beyond my eye
and marked my brain
with what is right
and what is just insane

no more hands wrung
put an end to sighing
grant me no lofty plans
to fill the time I'm buying

let me see that feeble thread
which binds each leap and bound
holding me to what's been said
chaining me to common ground

deep in the games of men
I see that sword and pen
both claiming they have won
agree to turn their backs again

Unto Us Is Born...

a hairline crack betrays
the folded life within
spreads out its delta
to embrace
to pacify
the throb

fragments cannot curb
the indignant beak
bursting
skyward
full of limp power
with tacky eyes homed
in on shattered safety
it plummets to inertia

a feeble wing
still wet with living glue
tries to wipe
away the womb

piece by piece
the dreadful secret
is forced down
the virgin gullet
to lie deep
and double crossed
inside

the fledgling struts
denial shakes
the forest floor
whilst the wind betrays the confessional
whispering all
to feeble-minded trees

The Estate Agent's

face pressed
against
the frosted glass
of real-estate
he scans the board
for a vacant lot
of promised land
to let

an unmarked square
on which to build
a temple
or a shack
to unfurnish
and
move in

to live
unlisted
for a while
to keep his breath
a secret there
and

will his heart
to beat the hunters
from his door